POEMAS DE BUEN AMOR ...
Y A VECES DE FANTASÍA

POEMS OF GOOD LOVE ...
AND SOMETIMES FANTASY

ACKNOWLEDGEMENTS

Colophon in Spanish edition (tr. JC):

Printing was finished today
Sunday, June 29, 1969, of
this book of love poems
first to last by the author
and under his care,
in collaboration with
pressman Narciso Perdomo
platemaker Rosendo Gálvez
at NUEVO MUNDO PRESS
65 Calle Arzobispo Meriño
in the city of Santo Domingo
and in the Dominican Republic.

The translator expresses deep gratitude to fellow translators Sharon Dolin and Gregary Racz and especially Rhina Espaillat and David Unger for their helpful suggestions, as well as to members of Barbara Harshav's translation group for theirs; to Daniel Deutsch for his critical feedback on the preface; to David Rosenthal for his beautiful translation of Lope de Vega's "Various Effects of Love", originally published in *Unsplendid* (4.1), from which the closing tercets that appear in the introduction are taken; and to Celeste Mir, daughter of the poet, for her enduring support and her invaluable help with the realization of this book. Grateful acknowledgement is made to the following magazines for prior publication: *Asymptote* ("Invitation", "Sonnet of the Grateful Girl", "Seafaring Date with an Imaginary Woman", "Residence in Fruit"); *Massachusetts Review* ("Demand of the Centuries"); *Poetrybay* ("Sonnet of the Young Girl", "Sonnet of the Pure Girl", "Sonnet of the Pregnant Girl").

PEDRO MIR

POEMAS DE BUEN AMOR ...
Y A VECES DE FANTASÍA

POEMS OF GOOD LOVE ...
AND SOMETIMES FANTASY

TRANSLATED BY JONATHAN COHEN

INTRODUCTION BY SILVIO TORRES-SAILLANT

PEEPAL TREE

First published by Nuevo Mundo Press
Santo Domingo
The Dominican Republic in 1969
This translation first published
in Great Britain in 2023
Peepal Tree Press Ltd
17 King's Avenue
Leeds LS6 1QS
UK

ISBN 13: 9781845235604

Printed in the United Kingdom
by Severn, Gloucester,
on responsibly sourced paper

MIX
Paper from
responsible sources
FSC
www.fsc.org   FSC® C022174

CARBON
NEUTRAL

Supported using public funding by
ARTS COUNCIL
ENGLAND

CONTENTS

Pedro Mir around the time of these poems.

SILVIO TORRES-SAILLANT

INTRODUCTION:
THE TRIUMPH OF ART OVER DOGMA

Jonathan Cohen's dexterous English rendition of Pedro Mir's least accessible volume of verse *Poemas de buen amor ... y a veces de fantasía* (1969) succeeds remarkably at making the poet's difficulty available in a way which does justice to the book's reticence to speak plainly. Cohen here achieves a major feat of enabling pure communication by conveying the opacity of Mir's Spanish original in an English version that renders the elusiveness legible without turning it into clarity. The translator enables the reader to appreciate the density of Mir's utterance, respecting his choice to withhold access to his unsayable feelings and thoughts. The renowned poet and fine translator Rhina P. Espaillat, who first spoke Spanish in her native Dominican Republic before migrating to English in New York City schools from 1939 onwards, has recently attested to the challenge of treating the incomprehensible with respect as she pondered on the task of translating a collection of poems by New York-based Dominican immigrant painter, poet, and performance artist Jimmy Valdez-Osaku, whose verse she at first found impenetrable. In her preface to her translations appearing in his *Creative Exile* (2020), Espaillat speaks of the poet's utterance as one that demanded of her a new literacy: "Having composed poems, from the age of four, using the tools of the speaker, singer, dancer, drummer wielding the percussion of meter and substitution, sound repetition of all kinds, theme and variations, and all of what the body does with language, I'm learning a different syntax, a grammar that has to be not so much heard and decoded as smelled and tasted, to process experience via sensation and memory, with only minimal mediation from common speech." I imagine Cohen's rapport with the untranslatable moments in Mir's work to have been not entirely unlike what Espaillat reports about translating Valdez.

As Anglophone readers who have encountered the poetry of Pedro Mir (1913–2000) via Cohen's previous translations of his work would know, the reticence to say it plain is not among the features associated with the bard who remains the Dominican Republic's poet laureate two decades plus after his death. No living poet since has elicited nationwide acclaim of the kind that led a legislative consensus of the multi-partisan National Congress to bestow the title on him in the 1980s. Transparency, not obscurity, had earned him such an honour, the clarity with which his verse had captured the yearnings of the citizenry for a genuinely democratic social order with peace, justice, equality, and inclusion for all. Like no other Dominican poet before him, he had interpreted the national sentiment in a compelling way in language that, though ornate and stylized, accessibly conveyed its social tidings to readers and listeners across the spectrum of class, levels of schooling, and literary exposure.

The communication agenda of *Poems of Good Love*, then, appears to veer away from the dominant tenor of Mir's oeuvre, and the reason for the shift may lie in the ideological course of the book's aesthetic project. Here, the poet sets out to write love poetry in a way that accords with his Marxist worldview, to sing to Eros while observing the tenets of historical materialism. He tries to render love logical, concrete, and intelligible as a condition which takes place within parameters dictated by concrete human imperatives in time and space. The poet then avoids the otherworldliness and the ineffability that usually shrouds the idea of love in the European literary tradition: say, as Catullus sings to Lesbia, Petrarch to Laura, or Ronsard to Cassandre. In this tradition, the male speaker evokes a lady who seldom acquires the materiality of a woman made of flesh and bone. Until *Poems of Good Love*, as German E. Ornes recorded two years after its publication, Mir had intentionally stayed away from love poetry on the grounds that the subject had to do with the rapport between "two individuals" and that, as it pertained to the realm of "private lives", it did not fit the *social* ambition of his "poetic project."

Cognizant that love mattered to all of humanity, Mir tried to tackle the "universality" of the subject in *Poems of Good Love* by approaching it in a manner that would concur with his materialist vision. He thus proceeded to break with the long tradition of love poetry that in his view had failed to re-create the tangible reality of the beloved, including the verse of innovative modern poets such as Pablo Neruda, who, he believed, had innovated mostly at the level of form, as he explained in his 1974 interview with Guillermo Piña Contreras. He, therefore, retains traditional forms in *Poems of Good Love*, as we can see in three sonnets that follow shortly after the "Dedication" at the start of the volume. When it came to elements of prosody, Mir dismissed the dichotomous framing of the rapport between the old and the new in literary commentary. Suggesting that it is its application that lends currency to a poetic form, he sustained in an earlier interview that "the old can be inserted in the new at a higher level of development, as new, with a new content; in other words, a sonnet or a madrigal written in the twentieth century, with the same metrical requirements as in days of old, has a different sense if it captures the drama of our time" (*La Gaceta Literaria de Auditorio*, 1972).

Mir's conforming with harmonizing the old and the new explains the musicality and the occasional rhyme schemes in *Poems of Good Love* that hark back to classical Spanish poetry. Similarly, his choice of title for his volume seems deliberate in its intent to evoke *El libro de buen amor* (*The Book of Good Love*), the ribald and formally mixed poem in the *mester de clerecía* (ministry of clergy) tradition written by the Castilian cleric Juan Ruiz (c. 1283–1350), known as Archpriest of Hita for the position that he held in the clergy at Hita. The Archpriest's poem combines allegory with devotional poetry and a first-person narrative evocation of a man's quest for true love, which he pursues through a serial seduction of women from across the social spectrum, ranging from a nun to a baker. In so far as he sets on a quest, a path of discovery, *The Book of Good Love* follows a less rigid poetic project than does *Poems of Good Love*; hence the ambivalence we find in the medieval text between the profane and the sacred, the flesh and the faith, grace and desire.

Mir's text, on the other hand, has an ideology and a philosophy of history to comply with. As he composed his volume, the poet followed the conviction that "the ultimate aim of love is not poetry but the procreation of human beings", as he told Piña Contreras. Consequently, the poems in his collection set out not to discover but to demonstrate a thesis. In it love equals carnal desire since it is such desire that brings two bodies to copulation as a prelude to the conception that procreation requires. The pages of the volume, then, privilege the pull of carnal appetite and consummation more than we find in the verse of Juan Ruiz, which primarily stressed the art of seduction. Mir's lovers obey the biological injunction that courses through their veins, urging them to sexual intercourse. In the collection's second poem, the speaker tells of "an imaginary woman" whom he met at the beach, where they heeded the erotic command: "Something like a well-timed shipwreck / shuddered in our veins — and then / closing our eyes tight and being swept away / we're suddenly conjugating the verb sand." In the second of three sonnets that follow, the consummation results in the young woman's defloration, which in the closing tercet the speaker confirms thus: "wearing the knapsack I had for my trip, / I said to myself at the threshold of her hips: / 'No lover yet has ever passed through here …'." By the same token, in the third sonnet in the triad, the speaker reports the material result of the intercourse, namely pregnancy and childbirth: "And thus I uncovered him, otherwise / asleep on a story, as his breath turned, / a little boy / with my brown eyes." The volume's most succinct expression of its procreative view of love — materialized as sex — comes in the poem "Demand of the Centuries", in which the speaker seeks to entice the beloved into carnal relations by explicitly voicing the desire to impregnate her: "Open your two ways / of gliding / on a tangent of the planet / and show me how to make people."

If Mir's poetic project entailed the ambition of novelty at the level of content, the resolve to render love material by stressing its consubstantiality with procreation-oriented sex may have actually failed to yield its intended revolutionary outcome. *Poems of Good Love* subscribes to a notion of love that leaves no room for same-sex intimacy and upholds the patriarchal model of affect that assigns to males the role of active initiators while relegating women to the rank of passive objects of men's amorous advances. Also, embracing the cult of virginity, it reproduces the pattern wherein the male lover achieves his fullest fulfillment in the knowledge of having been the first to have tasted the fruits a woman's body without expectation of bringing similar carnal innocence to their romantic encounter. The *niña* (girl) poems in the collection (sonnets to the "Young Girl", "Pure Girl", and "Pregnant Girl") may elicit suspicion among readers in the third decade of the twenty-first century who may be acutely aware of the threat looming over underage girls from predatory adult males. But the *girlhood* of the beloved invoked in those poems refers to a moment prior to carnal initiation rather than her chronological age. The virginity cult favours a language that names a female's maturation in terms of her intimate relations with men as a sort of rite of passage, sexual intercourse being the vehicle whereby she moves from *girl* to *woman*. The Latin American popular songbook teems with lyrics that evoke this transition of the beloved via intimate relations with the male speaker.

To transcend the limitations that the cult of virginity imposes on intimate relations, Mir's historical materialism would have had to pair up with a vision of gender equity, an ideological step that Latin American Marxists of his generation seldom took, confident as they were that the class struggle sufficed to address all other aspects of social injustice. Similarly, the very close tie between sex and procreation puts Mir in the company of very unlikely predecessors, such as the conventional sexual mores of Catholicism and other patriarchal religions. Benjamin Franklin, a North American sage who had no quarrel with his patriarchal status quo, included "Chastity" among the 13 virtues he advised to those wishing to live morally. Endorsing a near-celibate practice, he discouraged "venery" except "for health or offspring, never to dullness, weakness, or the injury of your own or another's peace or reputation." His

Autobiography offers no hint to indicate whether Mrs. Franklin shared his view on this "virtue."

Overall, *Poems of Good Love* is a triumph of imagination and verbal dexterity as Mir sets out to craft various scenes of couples engaged in the otherwise ordinary act of copulation in the effort to enact his theory of the materiality of love. The Spanish Golden Age poet Lope de Vega (1562–1635) had tackled the subject of love in "Varios efectos del amor" ("Various Effects of Love"), a sonnet which seems to posit that one can better explain love through the contradictory "effects" it can have on us than through any rational understanding. The closing tercets convey the spirit of the whole: "To face away from disillusionment, / to swallow venom like liqueur, and quell / all thoughts of gain, embracing discontent; / to believe a heaven lies within a hell, / to give your soul to disillusionment; / that's love, as all who've tasted know too well" (tr. David Rosenthal).

Similarly, among the most compelling texts in *Poems of Good Love* is "Salute to Love", a piece that relinquishes the epistemic authority of the book's "poetic project", seeming to surrender to the old notion of love as mystery and overwhelming feeling that defies reason, subverting Mir's own materialist theory and consorting with the love poetry tradition ancient and modern. Its lines exhibit a striking kinship with the spirit of Lope's sonnet: "Thanks to you I now know the ultimate / ... / the pleasure of suffering, equally / as much as imposing suffering. / ... the ultimate / tremor of my adventurous body / and the pleasure of biting / and the pleasure of dying. / ... / Thanks to you I now know hatred. / I salute you." Since Marx himself believed that great art transcends the ideology of its creators, one can speculate that Mir would not have been shocked by a reading that finds him as a poet contradicting his own political dogma. It may be that the discursive opacity of *Poems of Good Love* reflects Mir's own hunch vis-à-vis the tenets that informed the volume. The collection's lesser transparency in relation to the rest of the poet's oeuvre involves the content no less than the form, and we ought to be grateful to Jonathan Cohen for having rendered the opacity of both digestible to an Anglophone readership.

JONATHAN COHEN

TRANSLATOR'S PREFACE:
RE-CREATING MIR'S LYRIC VOICE

Translating Pedro Mir's love poems into English is both a critical and creative challenge. It called to me because I admire him so much and think his poetry deserves more attention in the Anglophone world. That is why I have translated him in the past. Like all his work, these love poems are finely wrought constructions. The task for me was painful at times because discerning the exact meaning of certain words racked my brain, especially in surrealistic passages. The translator must often choose one over several possibilities. Not only that, the rhymes and metrics of the traditional poetic forms that Mir uses so beautifully, as in his sonnets, are impossible to re-create in perfectly equivalent fashion without padding and wild interpolations. Translation of them, at best, is an approximation, and the reason to read them in Spanish. But at the same time, it still is possible to make real poems in English, using Mir's work as a blueprint, that are faithful to his verse. Poems that give English-speaking readers the experience of the potent lyricism and originality of his voice. Poems that sound like him and convey his intent. This has been my goal.

Poems of Good Love . . . and Sometimes Fantasy is a wonderful book of erotic love poetry, very different from the bardic political poetry largely associated with Mir. Here, he is not the poet of the people — the famed Whitman of the Caribbean — crying out for social justice. These poems are personal. In them he exposes his heart to a woman in pursuit of her, or he recollects the ecstasy of a love affair, or he wails over the agony of love lost. He shows in spades his capacity to love. He shows his bravado and machismo. He shows his weaknesses, failings, and anger, as much as he shows tenderness and his enduring quest to discover the way to love. The lyric quality of the poems is essential to them. My translation aims to embody that. Its music cannot replicate the music that Mir creates with Spanish, but the translated poems can reproduce the tonal movement of his words and lines, while their music must be created freshly in English.

Silvio Torres-Saillant points out that Mir complained modern love poetry differs from the old tradition only in form, but overall it has failed to portray the raw physical reality of love.* He, in contrast, retains traditional forms while daring to depict this reality. As the lover sings to the beloved in this book, we see reality in all its crude beauty. Mir said "el objetivo final del amor no es la poesía, sino la procreación de los seres humanos" ("the ultimate aim of love is not poetry, but the procreation of human beings"). And this concept, informed by a material view of the world, is clearly displayed in the book's poems. The scent of human flesh and the presence of carnal appetite run through them like a steady breeze. The idea of true love becomes very real with Mir. It informs the language of his poems and must infuse their translation. That was a central object of my work, to convey his open amorousness.

My approach to translating this book has been to achieve a poetic paraphrase; sometimes word for word, sometimes sense for sense (for instance, in "By Way of Introduction", the words literally meaning "understand each other" became "hear what we say" for the poetics of the line). I resisted changing Mir's opacity into clarity in order not to domesticate and betray the poems. Concerning diction, like Mir, I used natural colloquial language. I used organic form as he does in the poems written in free verse. I also used it in rendering those poems in traditional forms, creating end rhymes only where possible without gross distortion. Internal rhyme within lines, through assonance, helped re-create poetic structure. Use of

---

* Silvio Torres-Saillant, "Caribbean Poetics", PhD diss., (New York University, 1991).

cadence mostly, versus meter, facilitated the composition of lyrics in keeping with the song of each poem here. I followed the classic modernist principle promoted by Ezra Pound: "As regarding rhythm: to compose in the sequence of the musical phrase, not in sequence of a metronome." Ultimately, all pain a distant memory, I am happy with the outcome of the translation. I feel the poems are true to Mir in both letter and spirit, re-creating his voice in American English.

My confidence is based on my previous experience as a translator of Mir. His life and mine intersected in the mid-1980s when I started translating him. We became friends. He encouraged me to work as his translator, telling me that he thought my translations were the best English versions of his poetry. Concerning my translation of his epic "Contracanto a Walt Whitman" ("Countersong to Walt Whitman"), the first translation I ever showed him, he wrote me with great generosity: "Su traducción me ha fascinado. Sin ser literal, ni mucho menos, es tan fiel y conserva tanto el estilo mismo y en general el espíritu del poema, que a veces pienso que supera el original." ["Your translation fascinates me. Without being literal, not in the least, it is so faithful and preserves the very style and overall the spirit of the poem so much, that sometimes I think it surpasses the original."] It is with his firm support and encouragement from the past that I feel confident to meet the challenge of translating him.

Our bilingual book here presents the Spanish published in the original 1969 edition of *Poemas de buen amor ... y a veces de fantasía* issued by Nuevo Mundo in Santo Domingo. The image of the rose in the "Dedication" is taken from that edition, as it appears. My hope is this book will expand Mir's audience in the English-speaking world and help give him his proper stature, especially in the Americas that produced him. He is a giant of a poet, absolutely original, bold, innovative. His entire poetic canon, like his love poetry, affirms the profound heart and soul he put into words he crafted to give pleasure to others, to uplift them, as much as to fulfill his need to embrace life.

POEMAS DE BUEN AMOR ...
Y A VECES DE FANTASÍA

POEMS OF GOOD LOVE ...
AND SOMETIMES FANTASY

A MANERA DE INTRODUCCIÓN

Siempre en nuestras ventanas
hablamos desde lejos
la lluvia cae cantando
y no nos entendemos

Si llueve entre nosotros
es que no nos queremos
tienes miedo del agua
yo quizás tenga miedo

Y pues que cae la lluvia
sin que no nos mojemos
somos en las ventanas
dos corazones secos

Dos lanchas encalladas
dos extraños desiertos
somos como dos tardes
sólo que no llovemos

Mejor es que la lluvia
borre nuestro recuerdo
y un adiós y unas lágrimas
nos lluevan desde lejos

Y que nuestras ventanas
se alegren de lo nuevo
el fragor de la carne
el amor verdadero

BY WAY OF INTRODUCTION

Always at our windows
we speak from far away
the rain falls singing and
we don't hear what we say

If it rains between us
we don't love each other
you're scared of water
I might just be scared

And so the rain falls
without making us wet
we're a couple of dry
hearts at our windows

Two boats run aground
two strange deserts
we're like two afternoons
except we don't rain

It's better that raindrops
wash our memory clean
and a goodbye, a few tears
rain on us from far away

And that our windows
rejoice in what's new
the clamour of our flesh
true love overdue

"Toda la humanidad ama al que ama."
— Emerson

"All mankind loves a lover."
— Emerson

Dedicatoria

A una mujer
inexistente
ni material
ni maternal
sino desnuda

Este poemario
que es una teoría
o meditación
acerca de la materia
como secreto de flor

Dedication

*To a woman
who isn't real
or physical
or maternal
just naked*

*This book of poems
that is a theory
or meditation
on the subject like
a flower's secret*

CITA MARINERA CON UNA MUJER IMAGINARIA

La mar ardía en azules
con una blanca humareda.

Tú traías tu traje a espuma.
Yo mi pantalón a vela.

Olía toda la tarde
a pescadores y almejas.

A red y a goletas.

Algo como un naufragio oportuno
se estremeció en nuestra venas
y apagando los ojos y arrastrándonos
conjugamos de pronto el verbo arena.

SEAFARING DATE WITH AN IMAGINARY WOMAN

The sea burned in blues
with a white cloud of smoke.

You wore your foamy dress.
I my sailing pants.

The whole afternoon smelled
of clams and fishermen.

Of netting and schooners.

Something like a well-timed shipwreck
shuddered in our veins — and then
closing our eyes tight and being swept away
we're suddenly conjugating the verb sand.

SONETO DE LA NIÑA JOVEN

Pues, la niña era joven, su alegría
era joven, su pecho diminuto
era joven y su ángulo de luto
era joven, más joven todavía.

Conocida que fue, como el minuto
contiene la dialéctica del día,
su mirada frutal la contenía
en cristal y en imágenes de fruto.

Sangre fina de fuego y rosas tiernas
en el tope de lirio de las piernas
suscitaban los vínculos y, pues,

conocida que fue, ardiendo y sola,
la noche la arrastró por la amapola
con un hombre enredado entre los pies.

SONNET OF THE YOUNG GIRL

Yes, the girl was young, her gaiety
was young, her near-flat chest
was young and her slouchiness
was young, even younger yet.

With her reputation, as the day's
dialectic contains a minute,
her fruitful looks contained her
in crystal and in images of fruit.

Fiery fine blood and tender roses
at the lily-shaped peak of her legs
aroused various bonds and, so,

with her reputation, hot stuff and lonely,
night carried her off through the poppies
with a man tangled between her feet.

SONETO DE LA NIÑA PURA

Era la forma pura. Con su extraña
gracia de hilar en la retina,
era la forma pura, vespertina,
vertiginosa de la telaraña.

Aunque encendía una peregrina
luz al crecer, era pura y huraña.
Yo carecía junto a una cabaña.
Ronsard iluminaba la colina ...

Era por tanto justa la experiencia.
Y, pues, al culminar su adolescencia
en el dorado ombligo, casi flor,

cargando mi mochila pasajera,
me dije en el umbral de su cadera:
— por aquí no ha pasado un solo amor ...

SONNET OF THE PURE GIRL

She was the pure kind. With a strange
charming way of spinning in her eyes,
she was the pure kind, the evening kind,
and she swiftly spun her silken web.

Although an eerie glow grew bright
and brighter, she was pure and shy.
I had no cabin there close by.
Ronsard washed the hill with light …

It was a fair two-way experience.
And, so, culminating her adolescence
on her golden navel, almost a flower,

wearing the knapsack I had for my trip,
I said to myself at the threshold of her hips:
"No lover yet has ever passed through here …"

SONETO DE LA NIÑA GRÁVIDA

Amaba. Toda ella consistía
en los rugidos de su erguido pecho.
Una mirada dirigida al techo.
Un adiós a las horas. Y era mía.

Solíamos gritar en un estrecho
pasadizo de eternidad y recibía
pulcra mi sangre, en su categoría
de mujer derribada sobre un lecho.

Pero ella amaba en toda su abundancia
natural y exhalaba una fragancia
su boca, de alelíes y de nardos.

Y ello fue que, dormido sobre un cuento,
le descubrí en la vuelta del aliento
un niño breve
                          con mis ojos pardos.

SONNET OF THE PREGNANT GIRL

She loved. She was all of herself
in the roaring of her erect breasts.
A gaze up toward the ceiling.
A goodbye to time. She was mine.

We used to scream on a narrow
ridge of eternity and she received
my faultless blood, in her state
as a woman toppled in bed.

But love she did in all her natural
abundance and her mouth exhaled
a fragrance like violets and tuberoses.

And thus I uncovered him, otherwise
asleep on a story, as his breath turned,
a little boy
             with my brown eyes.

EL PEREGRINO

La vida está violeta.
Tiene su vértigo en torno.
Ella era juego nocturno,
ella era naipe de oro.
Es
todavía.
Y amo este naipe sonoro.

Caminante en su camino,
arrancado del este azucarero
de un país muy aparte
pero mío …

La estrella cae callada
mientras le habla el peregrino:

— ella se llama flámula y fulgura,
— ella se llama llama y resplandece,
— ella se llama mía y se desnuda,
— me parece …

La vida está violeta.
Toda de estrellas de olvido.
Ella era naipe canoro
vuelto y revuelto en su nido.
Era
y lo es para siempre.

Y amo su naipe escondido.

THE PILGRIM

Life is violet.
It has its dizzying turns.
She was a nighttime game,
she was a golden card.
She still
is.
And I love this tuneful card.

Wayfarer on his way,
torn from the sugary east
of a country far off
but mine …

The star falls quietly
while the pilgrim speaks to her:

"she's called a pennant and shines,
"she's called a flame and glows,
"she's called mine and undresses,
"I think …"

Life is violet.
All the stars of oblivion.
She was a songful card
turned and shuffled in her nest.
She was
and she is forever.

And I love that hidden card.

LA NOCHE

Era la oscuridad crujida
de sospechosas manos.
Apenas, en mi corazón,
vagabundeaba un demorado susto.
Ella quizás dormía y mientras tanto
velaba entre sus muslos delicados
la sombra de un murciélago robusto.
Amenazaba el fuego
con rodear las colinas,
temblorosas,
del busto.
Y luego,
un rayo rosa de la madrugada
disipó mi figura y mi ternura.

Ella,
entre sueño y realidad,
amó la duda.

NIGHT

It was the rustling in the dark
of suspicious hands.
Just then, in my heart,
crept a slow-moving panic fright.
She maybe was asleep while I
watched over the shadow of a robust bat
between her delicate thighs.
Fire threatened
to surround the hills
of her trembling
breasts.
And then
a pink ray of morning's first light
dispelled my figure and my ardour.

She,
between dream and reality,
loved the doubt.

CONNUBIO

Un gato
ardía lo porvenir
con dos augurios.
Éramos entonces
tú
y yo.
Los días
venían con dos caminos ocultos.
Uno, que eras tú,
de aromas.
El otro, ya lo sabes,
de un insistido trazo taciturno.
Cuando hizo la sombra su equipaje
yo te dije:

  — Guárdame entre tus besos
  este último.

E hicimos
de dos augurios
uno
único.
Hicimos
de dos caminos secretos
sólo uno.
En las sombras
el gato se detuvo.
Los días
anudaron su semblante
y aquel beso camina por el mundo.

MARRIAGE

A cat
set the future ablaze
with two omens.
Back then we were
you
and I.
The days
came with two hidden roads.
One, which was you,
so fragrant.
The other, you know, me
so insistently aloof.
When the shadow packed its bag
I told you:

> "Among your kisses,
> keep this last one for me."

And we made
two different omens
into a single
one.
We made
two secret roads
into just one.
The cat paused
in the shadows.
The days
strung their faces together
and that kiss now roams the world.

SONETO DE LA NIÑA AGRADECIDA

— Niña, ¿dónde tú vas?

                       — A los jazmines.

— ¿Sin besos?

               — Con mi boca en la mañana.

En sus ojos hervía la solana.

En mi sangre lloraban los clarines.

— ¿Y tú?

           — Donde tú estés.

                    — ¿Y tu manzana?

— En ti.

        Ya estaba en mí. De los jardines

de su aliento brotaban los jazmines

y en su cuerpo rugía la solana.

Con sol y soledad, en una alfombra

mínima de su vértice de sombra

fui triunfo del jazmín que se degrada.

Hubo una tibia paz en su cadera …

— Niña, ¿dónde tú vas?

                    — A donde quiera

que tu sombra me sirva de almohada.

SONNET OF THE GRATEFUL GIRL

"Babe, where you going?"

                  "To the jasmines."

"No kiss?"

        "With my mouth in the morning."

Sunshine flared in her eyes.

Bugles were crying in my blood.

"And you?"

       "Wherever you are."

               "And your apple?"

"In you."

      It already was in me. Jasmines
bloomed sweetly in the gardens of her breath
and sunshine roared in her body.

With the sun and solitude, on a tiny rug
lying there by its corner of shade
I won out over the jasmine that withers.

There was a warm peacefulness on her hip …
"Babe, where you going?"

           "Wherever you want
where your shade can be my pillow."

SONETO ESCRITO SOBRE LAS ALAS DE UNA MARIPOSA

Cuartetos:

Tú. Inédita y nocturna como un libro.

Tercetos:

Yo. Guardado para siempre entre tus páginas.

SONNET WRITTEN ON THE WINGS OF A BUTTERFLY

Quatrains:

You. Unedited, nocturnal like a book.

Tercets:

Me. Forever saved between your pages.

LA DEMANDA DE LOS SIGLOS

Sílfide bronca y espléndida
animal absoluto,
abre tus dos maneras
de caminar
sobre una tangente del planeta
y enséñame a poblar.
A convertir en caras las penínsulas,
en marinos los archipiélagos,
en horizontes mágicos
tu estilo redondo
de caminar.
Abre tus dos equilibrios
como las páginas de un libro
que enseña a poblar
y enséñame a darle forma
a una pequeña
nariz, piel a unos huesos,
a una sonrisa el matiz
de pequeño azul en que termina
tu tendón más externo
y más tierno
para hacerme absolutamente animal,
bronco animal absoluto
y eterno.

DEMAND OF THE CENTURIES

Wild and splendid Sylph
you absolute animal,
open your two ways
of gliding
on a tangent of the planet
and show me how to make people.
To turn peninsulas into faces,
archipelagos into sailors,
into magical horizons
your circular manner
of gliding.
Open your two scales
like the pages of a book
that shows how to make people
and show me how to form
a small flesh
nose, skin for some bones,
for a smile with the touch
of a little blue where
your outermost and softest
tendon ends
to make me absolutely an animal,
an absolute wild animal
that lives forever.

DÉCIMA

Por fin que tuvo un recado
para tí la ventolera.
Era en los árboles y era
en tu muslo redondeado,
en tu pelo deshojado,
y en tu mirada café.
El recado no lo sé
pero sé tus labios fríos,
tus rudos escalofríos
y el árbol bajo el que fue.

DECIMA

At last a raw gust of wind
had a message just for you.
It was in the trees and it was
in the roundness of your thigh,
in your leafless winded hair,
and in your coffee-brown look.
I don't know the message
but I do know your cold lips,
your sharp chills and the tree
under which it went finally.

INDICATIVOS DEL RETORNO

Por aquí

    se nace de una sola vez

Por aquí

    se domina el paisaje
    las flores giran su delgado sentido

Por aquí

    se desciende al abismo
    se aprende a llorar
    o a rondar por el vértigo

Por aquí

    se llegar al amor
    y al desatino

Y aquí se muere de algunos besos

SIGNS OF RETURN

Over here

    you are born in one shot

Over here

    the landscape takes over
    flowers twirl their slender meaning

Over here

    you descend into the abyss
    you learn to cry
    or wander feeling dizzy

Over here

    you arrive at love
    and foolishness

And here you die of some kisses

DESPUÉS DE HABERLA SEGUIDO

Después de haberla seguido
por años y por ciudades
que tenían su mismo
perfil y su distancia misma,

primero;

después de haberla tenido
al alcance de la mano
como un cazador que contempla
una torcaz en dirección del rifle,

segundo;

después de haberla sostenido
como un puente y haber hecho
pasar debajo de ella los riachuelos
lunares que laten con el pulso,

tercero;

se sentó junto a una piedra pensativa
y escribió este poema que intitula:

MEMORIAS DE UN SUICIDA INVOLUNTARIO

Y se puso a morir de gratitud.

AFTER HAVING PURSUED HER

After having pursued her
for years and through cities
that possessed her same
profile and her very distance,

first;

after having had her
within arm's reach
like a hunter who beholds
a dove in the sight of his rifle,

second;

after having supported her
like a bridge and having made
lunar streams pass under her
pulsing on their way,

third;

he sat down by a pensive stone
and wrote this poem he titles:

MEMORIES OF AN INVOLUNTARY SUICIDE

And he started to die of gratitude.

MUCHEDUMBRE

Ella
quería que en sus brazos
cupieran todos los hombres
como en los mapas azules
cabe el universo.
Tenía tantos años
como dedos de rosa.
Eso
lo explica todo. Y además
sus muslos terminaban
en el reino del pez
y la unidad.

El Hombre
estaba entonces maduro
para toda la verdad.

Y al tocar a la puerta
de sus desnudos peces
se prodigó en tal número
de formas abolibles
sobre la cuenca del muslo,
sobre la concha del párpado,
sobre la curva del cuello
hasta el sello y el cráter
de su nocturnidad,
que el Hombre mismo le entregó los hombres,
todos los hombres juntos,
juntos y cejijuntos,
de la Humanidad.

MASSES

She
wanted all mankind
to fit in her arms
as the universe
fits on blue maps.
She was as old
as rose fingers.
That
explains everything. And
her thighs went up to
the kingdom of fish
and unity.

Man
was then old enough
for all the truth.

And knocking on the door
of her naked fishes
such a number
of diminished forms appeared
in the cave of her thighs,
on the shell of her eyelid,
on the curve of her neck
up to the stamp and crater
of her nocturnity,
that Man himself gave her mankind,
all people together,
masses with brows knit together
of Humanity.

ANUNCIACIÓN DE LA PALOMA

Alba perdida para la mirada.
— No.
               Pido tu boca de naranja oprimida.
— No, tus ojos resbaladizos caen
sobre las palomas pertenecidas
y no, no, no.
              Pero es sólo la sombra de una mirada ...
— Pues, no.

Así empezaron nuestros amores
de aquella manera clara.
Yo deleitando la savia prometida,
tú resistiéndola un poco derramada.

Y cuando era imposible para tu boca
decir lo que no y adolecía
y apremiaba rigores de naranja
mis palomas volaron hacia ti
y te inundaron de sorpresas blancas.

ANNOUNCEMENT OF THE DOVE

Dawn lost to sight.
"No."
                    I ask for your mouth like an orange to squeeze.
"No, your slippery eyes fall
upon the pigeons you own
and no, no, no."
                    But it's just the shadow of a look …
"Still, no."

That's how our love affair began
in that clear way.
I delighting in the promised sap,
you resisting it, a little spilled.

And when it was impossible for your mouth
to say whichever no and I suffered
and rushed to twists of orange
my doves flew right to you
and flooded you with white surprises.

RESIDENCIA EN LA FRUTA

¿Aceptas que me diste residencia
en el mismo interior de una fruta?
Sucedió
en el momento de un escalofrío.
Allí te consagré todos mis glóbulos
inclusive el más débil,
el último que se arranca,
el que no vuelve jamás
sino en sabor de raíces amargas.
Si fue en un escalofrío,
¿Cómo pudo ser tan duradero, cómo
pudo ser inolvidable
sin prolongarse más?

RESIDENCE IN FRUIT

Will you admit you gave me a home
in the very inside of a fruit?
It happened
at the moment of a shiver.
There I pledged all my blood cells to you
including the weakest,
the last to escape,
the one that never comes back
except in the taste of bitter roots.
If it was in a shiver,
how could it last so long, how
could it be unforgettable
without lasting longer?

PENSAMIENTO QUE NO LLEGA A PALABRA

Jamás trenzaré nuestro pasado
Jamás destrenzaré nuestro futuro
ni lo que pudo haber sido del recuerdo
ni lo que aún puede ser de la esperanza
sino el presente
este presente
este mar
que eres tú
del que no quiero flotar
sino permanecer
en el fondo profundo
en el fondo más hondo
en el último fondo
para siempre
jamás

THOUGHT THAT DOESN'T ATTAIN A WORD

I will never twine our past
I will never untwine our future
or what might have become a memory
or what may still be hoped for
but the present
this present
this sea
that you are
I don't want to float from
but to remain
deep down
deepest down
at the final depth
forever and
always

INVITACIÓN

Te ofrezco para empezar
          un bouquet de palabras
como lámina y lumbre y borbollar de la fuente.
Después te doy el calor de mis manos
para el escalofrío de tu vientre.
Después te doy la composición de mi sangre
recorrida por todos los viaductos del oxígeno
y la cal y la nervadura de mis dientes.
Y además mi alimento
          mi yodo y mi magnesio
mi fósforo y mi sal
          mi albúmina y mi arena.
Y más te doy
          mi rostro diluido
a la temperatura de mis genes
o mis gentes.

Y tú no tendrás nada más que recibir
y eternizar
y acaso sollozar en el momento breve
para dejar constancia de que ya
de que ya estás salvada del olvido
y eres invulnerable para la muerte.

INVITATION

To begin I offer you
          a bouquet of words
as an illustration and firelight and bubbling of a spring.
Then I give you the warmth of my hands
for the shiver of your belly.
Then I give you the chemistry of my blood
coursed through all the viaducts of oxygen
and the lime and nerves of my teeth.
And in addition my nutrients
          my iodine and my magnesium
my phosphorus and my salt
          my albumin and my sand.
And plus I give you
          my face dissolved
at the temperature of my genes
or my folks.

And you won't need anything more to receive
and keep forever
and maybe sob over for a brief moment
so as to acknowledge that now
that now you are saved from oblivion
and you are invulnerable to death.

ESCÁNDALO EN LA ALBERCA

Junto a una moza
de cintura de vidrio
cantaba el jardinero:

— ¡Las rosas
primerizas y primorosas
de la primavera!

Contestaba la rana:

— ¡Primaverizas,
primaverosas!

Con sus ancas robustas
trepaba el macho
sobre las vértebras
de música de la rana.

Y contestaba el jardinero:

— ¡Primaverrisas,
primaverranas!

Pero el escándalo era la abeja
sobre la flor.
Experta en polen, artesana del néctar
y ella misma criada en la dulzura
sin jamás entender qué es el amor.

SCANDAL AT THE POOL

Alone with a maid
with an hourglass waist
the gardener sang:

"First to bloom
and so very beautiful
roses of spring!"

The frog replied:

"Springwhores,
springroses!"

With his strong legs
the male climbed
upon her musical spine
to frog music.

And the gardener replied:

"Springroars,
springfrogs!"

But the scandal was the bee
upon the flower.
An expert in pollen, artisan of nectar
and raised on sweetness
without ever knowing what love is.

HISTORIA Y DESGRACIA CIERTA DE
UNA VIOLENCIA INCREÍBLE

La diminuta plántula
con raíces y raicillas
sudó su crecimiento femenino
librando en los reductos de la tierra
quién sabe qué batalla
de sustento
para abundarse en ella.

El labrador
la ayudaba a crecer
salvándola de ortigas y de estrellas
de orugas y gusanos
con pequeñas astucias
y palabras pequeñas,
y, cuando ya era una planta
robusta y verdadera,
cuando, con la gracia en el viento
y el placer en la fibra,
madura la madera,
el labrador
se estableció en el polen,
se estremeció en el clima,
y se acostó con ella.

TRUE STORY AND DISGRACE OF
INCREDIBLE VIOLENCE

The tiny seedling
with roots and root hairs
worked its female growth hard
fighting in strongholds of the earth
who knows what battle
of sustenance
in order to thrive in it.

The farmer
helped it to grow
saving it from nettles and stars
from caterpillars and worms
with little tricks
and small words,
and, when it finally became
a robust and true plant,
when, with grace in the wind
and pleasure in its fibre,
the wood matured,
the farmer
settled in its pollen,
shivered in the weather,
and lay down with it.

CANCIONCILLA

Solías ser frutal, señora mía
de levantado pecho turbulento
y desde luego de color de rosa.
Y desde luego de amapolas blancas
por lo imposible de las amapolas.
Pero en tus ojos retozaba el viento
y te arrancaba una mirada tórrida.
Yo en cambio retornaba al verso
y te ignoraba repitiendo a solas:

—— Guarda ¡oh pecho! tu pérfido verano
y déjame que solloce sobre tus frutas rojas.

LITTLE SONG

You used to be a fruit tree, darling
with your high unruly breasts
and of course with their pinkness.
And of course with white poppies
for the impossibility of poppies.
But the wind frolicked in your eyes
and it provoked a torrid look in you.
I, however, went back to my poem
and ignored you, repeating privately:

"Guard, oh breasts! your faithless summer
and let me sob over your red fruits."

SALUDO AL AMOR

Rosa vengativa, rosa
de cuello espinado, agudo.
Perfil de luna llorada.
Colina de brusco busto.
Paloma serena, cruel.
Por ti ya conozco el último
placer de saberlo todo:
el placer de sufrir iqual
que el de hacer sufrir.
Por ti ya conozco el último
temblor de mi cuerpo atrevido
y el placer de morder
y el placer de morir.
Por ti ya conozco el último
significado del odio.
Odio puro.
Por ti ya conozco el odio.

Te saludo.

SALUTE TO LOVE

Vengeful rose, that rose
with a sharp thorny neck.
Profile of a weeping moon.
Hill of sudden breasts.
Serene, cruel dove.
Thanks to you I now know the ultimate
pleasure of knowing all about it:
the pleasure of suffering, equally
as much as imposing suffering.
Thanks to you I now know the ultimate
tremor of my adventurous body
and the pleasure of biting
and the pleasure of dying.
Thanks to you I now know the ultimate
meaning of hatred.
Pure hatred.
Thanks to you I now know hatred.

I salute you.

ABOUT AUTHOR, TRANSLATOR, AND INTRODUCER

Pedro Mir (1913–2000) is recognised as the foremost poet of the Dominican Republic. Since publishing his first poems in 1937, he sought through literature to place the Caribbean experience in a global historical perspective. He also produced work in the fields of history, fiction, and art criticism and theory. In 1947, the subject of mounting suspicions of the Trujillo dictatorship, he was forced to go into exile. When he returned fifteen years later, following the death of the dictator, the poet immediately won the hearts of the Dominican people, and his poetry readings were mass public events attended by enthusiastic crowds of citizens from every walk of life. In 1982 the legislature of the Dominican Congress conferred upon him the title of National Poet, and in 1993 he received the National Prize for Literature, the highest honour a literary artist can receive in the Dominican Republic. On the occasion of his death, the president of the Dominican Republic declared three days of national mourning and celebrated Mir's memory and his work: "Don Pedro will always be with us because his thinking was transcendent, and he truly fathomed the national Dominican soul."

Jonathan Cohen is a poet, translator, essayist, and scholar of inter-American literature. He is the translator of Pedro Mir's *Countersong to Walt Whitman and Other Poems*, with Donald D. Walsh (Azul Editions, 1993; Peepal Tree Press, 2018), and *Two Elegies of Hope* (Spuyten Duyvil, 2019). Other translations include Ernesto Cardenal's *Pluriverse: New and Selected Poems* (New Directions, 2009), Enrique Lihn's *The Dark Room and Other Poems* (New Directions, 1978), and Roque Dalton's *Small Hours of the Night* (Curbstone, 1996). He is editor of William Carlos Williams's *By Word of Mouth: Poems from the Spanish, 1916–1959* (2011) and the "Centennial Edition" of Williams's *Al Que Quiere!* (2017) — both published by New Directions. His edition of Williams's translation of the Spanish Golden Age novella *The Dog and the Fever*, by Pedro Espinosa, was published in 2018 by Wesleyan University Press. For more information about Cohen's work, see jonathancohenweb.com.

Silvio Torres-Saillant is professor of English and Dean's Professor of the Humanities at Syracuse University. He is author of the introduction in Pedro Mir's *Countersong to Walt Whitman and Other Poems* (Azul Editions, 1993; Peepal Tree Press, 2018). His books include *Caribbean Poetics: Toward an Aesthetic of West Indian Literature* (Cambridge University Press, 1997; Peepal Tree Press, 2013), *The Once and Future Muse: The Poetry and Poetics of Rhina P. Espaillat*, with Nancy Kang (University of Pittsburgh Press, 2018), *An Intellectual History of the Caribbean* (Palgrave, 2006), and *The Dominican Americans*, with Ramona Hernández (Greenwood Press, 1998), among other works in both English and Spanish. A member of the editorial board of the University of Houston's Recovering the U.S. Hispanic Literary Heritage Project, he is associate editor of *Latino Studies* (Palgrave) and has edited the New World Studies Series for the University of Virginia Press.

ALSO BY PEDRO MIR

Countersong to Walt Whitman: A Bilingual Edition
Translated by Jonathan Cohen and Donald D. Walsh
ISBN: 9781845233563; pp. 198; pub. 2018; price £12.99

The eight poems selected include several of Pedro Mir's signature pieces from the late 1940s through the 1970s: "Countersong to Walt Whitman"; "There Is a Country in the World"; "If Somebody Wants to Know Which Is My Country"; "To the Battleship Intrepid"; "Not One Step Back"; "Amen to Butterflies"; "Concerto of Hope for the Left Hand"; "Meditation on the Shores of Evening." The introduction by Silvio Torres-Saillant, author of *Caribbean Poetics* (Peepal Tree Press), and foreword by Jean Franco, author of *Cruel Modernity* (Duke University Press), enable a broader appreciation of the personal context and general impact of Mir's work. A selected bibliography of works by and about the poet, including an accounting of the prose he has published as a novelist, author of short stories, essayist, and historian, provides readers with ample resources for further appreciation of Mir's achievement. As Torres-Saillant emphasizes: "The present bilingual edition ... will give both Spanish- and English-speaking readers ... the opportunity to recognize themselves in the poetic visage of one of the most authentic literary artists to have come from the Caribbean."

Roberto Márquez stated in the *Village Voice*: "The publication, in bilingual format, of this first book-length anthology of work by the Dominican Republic's internationally acclaimed and locally celebrated National Poet is an event — long anticipated, too long delayed ... Colleague, contemporary, and the equal in lyric vitality, epic ambition, and communal significance to Pablo Neruda or Nicolás Guillén, Mir remains, with Martinique's Aimé Césaire, perhaps the most masterfully elegant and majestic among the living voices of a generation that boasts more than its share of world-class poets ... [Mir's] poetry achieves a rare, exceptionally felicitous marriage of poetry and politics, of individual sensibility and the chronicling of quotidian collective drama, the still unfulfilled promise of Latin America, its landscape, peoples, and societies."